Contents

Tables

Preface

Negotiation is something we do everyday. In some way, shape, form or fashion, we all negotiate with the intent to get what we want. During the Negotiation as an Applied Theory research elective, my interest in negotiation peaked. I wanted to know more, and wanted to know how to be a master negotiator. At the same time, during research topic discussion, I had a hard time trying to tie negotiation into a "problem." I didn't want to necessarily do something with leadership or my career field. Instead, I wanted to do something "out of the box." This idea was suggested by the advisor, Dr. Eisen, as a possible research topic. The idea caught my attention, but it was more from the standpoint of "this is common sense, so surely someone has already addressed this topic." Surprisingly, I could not find anything on the topic of negotiation and interrogation together. Each time I brought the topic up to various individuals, I got the "hmm, never really thought of that; but it sounds interesting" response. So began my quest to tie the topic of negotiation and interrogation together.

I would like to thank Dr. Eisen for the idea and the Air Force Cultural Center to allow me to attend the Reid Technique of Interviewing and Interrogation Seminar. This seminar was a goldmine of information and well worth the 3 days of invaluable knowledge. I would also like to thank the assistance I received from the Army Military Intelligence personnel and the Office of Special Investigation personnel. Finally, I want to thank my friends that entertained my newfound interrogation techniques and allowed me to bounce ideas of them. It is my hope that each person who reads this paper is able to see the glaring correlation between interrogation and negotiation as clearly as I do. It is also my hope that interrogators actually begin to use the

iii

negotiation methods outlined in this paper and eventually a study will be conducted on the success rate using these "kindler, gentler" methods.

Abstract

This paper takes a look at the relationship between Reid's Technique of Interviewing and Interrogation and the theory of negotiations. During the last several years, interrogation is viewed in a negative light based on the incidents that occurred in Abu Gharib prison in Iraq and the alleged treatment of detainees in Guantanamo Bay, Cuba. This negative view created a negative connotation toward the word interrogation and prompted several policy changes within the Department of Defense. Negotiation, on the other hand, is something individuals do everyday and does not necessarily lend itself to a negative connotation. Negotiation and interrogation transactions take place everyday--on and off the battlefield and in and out of the boardroom. Negotiation and interrogation share several common themes and through a methodic approach, this paper highlights the commonalities between negotiation and interrogation. This paper analyzes the Reid Technique of interrogation and highlights the underlining negotiation theme throughout each step in the process. In the end, the two techniques share so many commonalities a negotiation style approach could be incorporated into interrogation techniques and make them for effective.

Introduction

In this day and age, the term interrogation is linked to a negative connotation. Many hear the word interrogation and immediately think of the harsh techniques used at Abu Gharib Prison in Iraq or the negative light shed on the detainee camp at Guantanamo Bay, Cuba (GITMO). Interrogation is usually linked to harsh tactics such as torture, mind games, sleep/food/water deprivation, and simulated drowning. It is these inhumane tactics that caused the POTUS to direct the closure of GITMO and also left a bitter taste in the mouth of Iraqis toward Americans. Interrogation does not have to be harsh. The old saying "honey attracts more flies than vinegar," is equally applicable for interrogations and negotiations. When people hear the word negotiation, they tend to think of "using what they have to get what they want." In an interrogation setting, the interrogator wants the subject to confess to something or tell the truth. The interrogator wants something the subject owns and uses what he/she can "to get what he/she wants." Negotiation and interrogation, although not commonly referred to together, share similar concepts and ideas. Incorporation of negotiation theory and practice into interrogation settings will yield better results.

The goal of this paper is to compare the interview and interrogation process to negotiation. The primary template for the interview and interrogation process is the Reid Technique, developed by John E. Reid in 1947. This paper analyzes the Reid 9-step process of interrogation and correlates each step to a negotiation practice or theory. The end result is a new way to look at interrogations and create a paradigm shift. Through a compare and contrast methodology, this paper outlines the glaring resemblance of negotiation and interrogation. This is not a new concept. Matthew Alexander, a key interrogator that led to the capture and ultimate

1

death of Abu Musab Al Zarqawi, did not use harsh techniques. He instead befriended the terrorists and used negotiation techniques to get the information he needed. It is the success of this operation in Iraq that led the military to emphasize a new approach to interrogation. Not an inhumane and torture-based approach, but instead one that uses humane tactics and treats the subject with respect.

If negotiation has been around forever, and the concept of using friendly techniques to make a subject talk in an interrogation is a tried and true practice, why were the two concepts never combined before? First, we must clarify some definitions and terms. There are two main levels of custody in interrogations—custodial and non-custodial. Custodial is generally related to an arrest or capture and the subject is deprived of his/her freedom to leave at any time. In custodial situations, Miranda must be given to the suspect.[1] The subject is there—normally against his/her will—and is under the interrogator's terms. Non-custodial is when the subject is not being held and is free to come and go at his/her will. For the purpose of this paper, the non-custodial aspect will be the primary focus, although there may be some reference to custodial aspects of interrogation.

What is interrogation? Reid defines interrogation as "an art whereby through the use of persuasion and observation the truth is elicited from a suspect by sound reasoning and understanding without the use of threats or promises."[2] The military definition of interrogation, according to FM 2-22.3, takes on a different approach and hence leads to the common misnomer of interrogation. It defines interrogation as "the systematic effort to procure information to answer specific collection requirements by direct and indirect questioning techniques of a person who is in the custody of the forces conducting the questioning."[3] By words alone, the military definition automatically denotes a custodial situation.

Let's take a look at the definition of negotiation. There is no one set definition of the word "negotiation," however this paper takes a few definitions into consideration. Gordon Rule defines negotiation as a "peaceable procedure for reconciling, and/or compromising known differences."[4] Cohen describes negotiation as a process where two or more parties work together to arrive at a mutually acceptable resolution of one or more issues.[5] One last definition of negotiation is "a process of combining conflicting positions into a common position."[6] At first glance, one may not see the correlation between interrogation and negotiation based on definition alone. Words like "peaceable procedure," "compromising," "combining conflicting positions into a common position," don't come to mind when the word interrogation is heard. However, interrogation is nothing more than negotiation. The scene and players are different, but the underlying goal is the same: to get something out of or from the other party involved. Approaching interrogation from a negotiation standpoint is "outside the box" thinking but it's precisely the type of thinking needed in order to break away from the negative definition of interrogation.

Background

Due to the evidence of abuse and the treatment of detainees in GITMO, as well as the Iraqi prison located at Abu Ghraib, interrogation techniques received a lot of bad press. For years, GITMO received public scrutiny due to the controversial interrogation techniques and the alleged abuse of detainees. GITMO was established in early 2002 as a detention camp to hold suspected terrorists that were captured in Afghanistan. These detainees were held for the duration of hostilities without being officially charged or tried for crimes. According to the US, these detainees are held in the interest of National Security and also act as a deterrent to prevent future attacks in the US.[7] Despite several allegations of enhanced interrogation techniques such

3

as waterboarding, prolonged solitary confinement, and exposure to extremes such as temperature, noise and light, the Pentagon insists that the detainees are treated humanely. According to White House spokesperson Tony Fratto, "Abuse of detainees has never been, is not and will never be the policy of this government. The policy of this government has been to take these detainees and to interrogate them, and get the information that we can get to help protect the country."[8] In 2002, guidelines were established for the treatment of detainees at GITMO. These guidelines were in line with "American values" and "to the extent appropriate and consistent with military necessity, in a manner consistent with the principles of the Geneva Convention."[9] Seventeen interrogation techniques were approved by the Secretary of Defense (SECDEF) in December 2002, but then rescinded in January 2003 due to concern on the implementation of some of the techniques.[10] Waterboarding was not approved, however there were three categories of techniques with category I being less severe and category III being most severe. Category II techniques included 20 hour interrogations, removal of a prisoner's clothing, standing for up to 4 hours, the use of dogs to frighten the detainees, isolation up to 30 days, deprivation of light, and forced shaving of the face and head.[11] The category III technique allowed mild physical contact such as grabbing, light pushing and poking in the chest as long as it didn't cause injury and was not applied maliciously or to intentionally cause harm.[12] The SECDEF made a comment on the Action Memo dated 27 Nov 02 that said, "however, I stand for 8-10 hours a day. Why is standing limited to 4 hours?[13] After a legal and policy review, 24 techniques were approved for use by the SECDEF in April 2003.[14] None of these techniques condoned torture.

The techniques approved in 2003 were for use in GITMO only. So what happened at the Iraqi detainee camp in Abu Ghraib? This is another highly publicized account of abuse and

4

wrongdoing. In an AR 15-6 Investigation of the Abu Ghraib Detention Facility, the major findings were lack of leadership oversight, lack of properly-trained interrogators, and a misunderstanding of doctrine and approved interrogation techniques.[15] The report states, on more than one occasion, that it was not the doctrine or lack thereof that caused the abuse situations. Instead, it was a case of some "morally corrupt and unsupervised soldiers and civilians."[16] In the report, there were 44 alleged instances of abuse on the detainees at Abu Ghraib. These abuses included direct physical assault to the point of unconsciousness, sexual posing, forced group masturbation, alleged rape and sexual assault.[17] Interrogation techniques such as the use of dogs, nudity, and isolation occurred; but none of these techniques were ever approved for use. One underlying problem appears to stem from the Military Intelligence (MI) personnel assigned to Abu Ghraib. These individuals were trained and familiar with the interrogation policy in Afghanistan and GITMO, and these individuals used the same training and policy at Abu Ghraib. There was no clear guidance on what interrogation techniques were allowed at Abu Ghraib, and there was no guidance on the type of treatment detainees could be subjected to. This laid the foundation for abuse and mistreatment to occur and it spread like wildfire from that point on. Eventually, the abuse incidents led to the closure of Abu Ghraib, but forever left a scar on the face of military interrogations.

It is precisely this reason that a paradigm shift must occur. In order to recover from the negative publicity of the past, it is imperative to take the lead of Matthew Alexander or Germany's most effective interrogator named Hanns-Joachim Schraff. Schraff was known for rarely raising his voice and creating the best conditions for detainees. He was nicknamed "the Master" for his ability to get information from suspects and many of his principles were incorporated into current military and CIA manuals.[18] These principles are simply the art of negotiation. A running joke between interrogators is "the only difference between a used car salesman and an interrogator is interrogators have to live by the Geneva Convention".[19]

Interviews versus Interrogations

Before interrogations begin, an interview should be conducted. Interviews are structured as information gathering sessions and are designed to be non-accusatory since guilt is normally uncertain at this point in time.[20] The interview is where the interrogator learns information about the subject and prepares the themes or arguments to use during the interrogation. The subject should do most of the talking and interviews can be conducted with minimal amounts of information and variable environments.[21] The interview stage is where the interrogator takes notes on the subject's verbal and non-verbal behavior. From this behavior, the interrogator builds rapport and finds some kind of common ground with the subject. In the Army Field Manual, this is called the approach.[22] The approach phase is where the interrogator sets the conditions and rapport in order to gain information from the subject. The objective is to establish a relationship that results in gaining accurate and reliable information in response to the interrogator's questions. An integral part of the approach phase is building rapport. The interrogator wants to build rapport with the subject in order to gain the subject's confidence which leads to willingness to cooperate.[23] The persona the interrogator presents to the subject is designed to evoke cooperation and, in turn, the subject responds with truthful, relevant information.[24] There are several different approaches that could be used in this phase, but it's important to keep in mind that whatever approach is used, the initial impression the interrogator makes on the subject will have a lasting effect on the ability to obtain information from the subject.

In negotiation, there are essentially three phases in the journey: information gathering, issue resolution, and decision making.[25] Information gathering is similar to the interview and approach phase. In this phase, the person learns all they can about the particular negotiation situation and the person or persons they are entering into negotiation with. The main purpose in this phase is to listen and get answers to specific questions prepared during the preparation phase.[26] Key information to gather during this information gathering is the other party's resources, issues, bargaining style, interests, needs, limits, alternatives, targets, goals, constituents, authority, social structure, reputation, style, strategy and tactics.[27] This information is obtained through direct and indirect questioning techniques between the negotiating parties, or it's obtained through research, friends, or business partners. It is also helpful to have an idea of past negotiation successes. A popular pre-negotiation tool is the interest map (IM) created by Steven Cohen. The IM offers a way to determine what information a negotiator needs, what questions to ask, what assumptions can be made, and what elements are available to help both parties reach a mutually satisfactory outcome.[28] An IM is fluid, and can be adjusted as the situation dictates and as interests change. In an IM, the stakeholders--or those concerned with the outcome of the negotiation—are identified and their interests and positions are listed. The IM helps identify connections between stakeholder's interests and helps guide negotiations in that the agreement should try to address as many stakeholder interests as practical.[29] An IM also describes the relationships between the stakeholders and helps identify impacts on one group as the result of changes in another. IMs help develop stakeholder priorities within their interests which gives the negotiator information as to what is the most and least important to each stakeholder.[30] Overall, this interest map is a tool for negotiators to evaluate to prepare for the actual negotiation process, plan the particular strategy, and help to guide the negotiations. An interest map is a roadmap to prepare for a negotiation or an interrogation. An IM when used as a planning tool in interrogation can allow the interrogator to focus on what is at stake and what possible outcomes could occur during the interview/approach/preparation phase.

Unlike interviews, interrogations are more interrogator-driven and take on a different tone. Interrogations are accusatory; the interrogator does most of the talking, projects an attitude that time is not limited, and finds out *why* the subject did something and not *if* they did it.[31] Interrogations should be conducted in a controlled environment and guilt should be reasonably certain before beginning the interrogation phase. The interrogator should not take notes until after they get a confession. The sole goal during the interrogation phase is to extract truthful admissions or confessions. The Reid Technique uses a methodical 9-step process to conduct interrogations. The 9 steps are: 1) Direct positive confrontation; 2) Theme development; 3) Handling denials; 4) Overcoming objections; 5) Procurement and retention of suspect's attention; 6) Handling the suspect's passive mood; 7) Presenting an alternative question; 8) Having suspect orally relate various details of the offense; and 9) Converting an oral confession into a written confession. These steps will be analyzed further in the paper. The thing to remember at this point is in order to proceed with the interrogation, the interrogator already analyzed all the information and reasonably suspects the person is guilty. Walker and Lewis, in their book *Six Steps to Negotiations Success*, identifies six steps to successful negotiations: 1) Analyze the negotiation situation; 2) Plan for the negotiation; 3) Organize for effective negotiations; 4) Taking control; 5) Closing negotiations; and 6) Continuous improvement.[32] The important thing to remember here is once the situation is analyzed, the negotiating parties will determine whether or not to proceed with the negotiation. Once the decision to continue with

8

negotiations is made, there is a methodical process involved that correlates similarly to the Reid 9-step interrogation process.

Characteristics of Successful Interviewers/Interrogators/Negotiators

As depicted in Table 1, there are similar characteristics between successful interviewers, interrogators and negotiators. Although negotiation is something done every day by everyone, it takes training and skill to become a consistently successful negotiator. It also takes skill and training to become a successful interviewer and interrogator.

Successful Negotiator	Successful Interviewer	Successful Interrogator
Be in full and complete charge	Objective attitude	Confident attitude
Able to make decisions	Nonjudgmental	Understanding
Assumes greater responsibility	Cordial and polite	Patient
Self-confident	Even-tempered	Upright posture
Sense of humor	Relaxed posture	Nonthreatening gestures
Positive thinker	Uncrossed arms	Understanding tone
Mental toughness	Conversational tone	Compassionate
Preparation & planning skill	Smooth speech	Responsive
Subject Matter Expert	No skeptical tone	
Think clearly/rapidly		
Listening skills		
Good judgment		
Intelligent		
Integrity		
Able to persuade others		
Patient		

Table 1[33]

Environment

Interviews and interrogations share common general themes: privacy and distraction-free. Based on the situation and the location, it's not always possible to have privacy and remove distractions. In these cases, it is imperative to create a sense of privacy and remove as many distractions as possible such as cell phones and interruptions. David Vessel, in his article "Conducting Successful Interrogations," states that "officers should not conduct interrogations unless they can guarantee privacy and control of the environment."[34] Ideally, interrogations are conducted in small, controlled-environment rooms that are free of windows, telephones, clocks, or intercom systems. Interrogations should take place between the interrogator and the subject, and outside of the view and hearing of third parties. In certain cases such as the use of a translator, for security, or with a partner, a third person may be required to be in the room. In these cases, the third person should be as little a distraction as possible.[35] There are several reasons for the emphasis on the two themes privacy and distraction-free. In a private and distraction-free setting, it forces the subject to respond to the questions and nothing else. Interruptions during an interrogation can break the interrogator's chain of thought and it gives the subject a chance to either stop talking or tell a lie.[36] In the next section, behavior symptoms are analyzed. The setting plays an important part of the behavior analysis because it allows the interrogator to better analyze the verbal and non-verbal behavior of the subject. If there are extra stimuli or distractions, it makes it hard to tell if the verbal and non-verbal behavior is due to deceit or to the distraction.

In negotiations, the location themes are not as stringent as in interrogation, however they serve the same purpose. The negotiation setting is agreed upon by both parties, but there are some inherent advantages and disadvantages. For example, if negotiations are being held between party A and party B at party A's location, party A has an advantage over party B. Party A controls the environment, much like the interrogator controls the environment over the subject. Party A can use this to his/her advantage and play against party B; or party A can use this to cater to party B. The setup of a room during negotiation can enhance the process, or detract from it. Most people are comfortable with one party on one side of the table and the other party on the other side of the table. Unintentionally, this type of setup creates a barrier. If the two negotiating parties tend to be busy, it would be wise to meet somewhere in private where there won't be any interruptions. Although not as strict as interrogations, essentially the same rules would apply regarding interruptions and telephones. The only way the phones would not be a distraction is in the case where a negotiating party needed to retrieve information or approval regarding the negotiation. Similar to a non-custodial interrogation, negotiating parties have the right to walk away at any time. In order to keep a negotiating party at the table, they must feel comfortable and not put at a disadvantage by the other party.

Behavior and Emotions

It is important to understand the role of emotion and behavior in both interrogations and negotiations. The non-verbal and verbal cues guide the outcome of each step in the interrogation and the negotiation process. During an interrogation, behavior determines the type of theme or approach to take with the subject, whether to move in, or whether to take a different approach.[37] Non-verbal behavior speaks louder than verbal and is normally harder to control. The body tends to answer truthfully, no matter what the mouth says. For example, a subject can say "no" with their mouth, but their head will shake "yes." Most times, an innocent person is genuinely truthful and does not have to fake truthfulness. On the other hand, a deceitful person tries to play the role of an innocent person and constantly thinks about what the innocent person would say or

11

do.[38] As the anxiety of the subject increases, so do their behavior symptoms. According to the behavioral symptom analysis used by the Reid Technique, a truthful subject tends to be unyielding and persistent in their denials during an interrogation.[39] A deceptive subject tends to be apologetic, "Um, sorry, wish I could help you out," and quiet.[40] Nonverbal symptoms of a truthful suspect include an upright, open and relaxed body posture and their gestures appear sincere and naturally timed.[41] Deceptive subjects have a slouched body posture or may appear frozen with rehearsed gestures that don't appear natural.[42] Overall, verbal and non-verbal behavior plays a huge part in interrogations. It's important for the interrogator to remain calm, patient, and non-judgmental during interrogations. Anything the interrogator does may have an effect on the subject and could jeopardize the opportunity to extract information.

The same concept applies to negotiations. Emotion and verbal/non-verbal behavior play a huge role at the negotiation table. In *How to Read a Person Like a Book*, the author argues one can learn a lot by facial expressions and posture alone. Confidence, boredom, expectancy, frustration, suspiciousness, readiness, and defensiveness are easily identified by the way a person sits, glances, smirks, tilts their head, crosses their arms, where they sit, and certain types of breathing patterns.[43] In negotiations, like interrogations, hot-button items are normally discussed and at times there are quite a few things on the line. Emotions and behavior can hurt or help the process. Properly inserted and managed, emotions and behavior can have a positive effect on the negotiation process. However, if emotion is not properly managed, it can lead to outbursts of anger, rage, and ultimately unwillingness in one or both negotiating parties. First, negotiating parties must recognize their emotions and understand their emotions as legitimate.[44] Each party should understand that emotions are part of negotiating and they should plan their reaction to certain issues that may arise through the negotiation process. Second, negotiators should remain focused on the problem and not the person.[45] Whenever emotions come up, it's important to stay focused on the overall objective—to reach an agreement both parties can live with. If the parties think of negotiating in a collaborative way—solving a problem before them and not between them—the likelihood of reaching an agreement increases.[46] Daniel Shapiro identifies two emotional goals during negotiations: affective satisfaction and instrumental satisfaction.[47] In affective satisfaction, a person is satisfied with the affect their emotion had on the other party. If the other party is happy, it makes the negotiator happy and they feel satisfied. On the flip side, if the other party is not happy, it leaves the negotiator with a dissatisfied affect.[48] Instrumental satisfaction deals with the extent to which parties are able to effectively and efficiently agree on the commitments they aspire to achieve.[49] In negotiations, positive emotions are linked to more integrative outcomes with less aggressive techniques. Positive emotions foster creative problem solving, exploration of ideas, and empathy towards the other party. Negative emotions foster inaccurate judgment and loss of focus on the overall objective. These emotions can lead to a more distributive or competitive situation and less integrative. In distributive bargaining, the goals of one party are usually in direct conflict with the goals of the other party.[50] This type of negotiation is known as competitive or "win-lose." It's a competition to see which party is going to get the most out of the deal.[51] Finally, it's important to realize sometimes positive emotions lead to negative results and negative emotions sometimes lead to positive results. Some negotiators try to elicit a certain response from the other party for strategic gain.[52] They can also use their own emotion and expression to elicit a certain response. For example, a party may feign anger or disgust over an offer made by another party in hopes to get the party to give in.[53] Manipulating emotions for strategic gain may get results in the beginning, but this type of

13

manipulation jeopardizes long term relationships.[54] Long term relationships may not be important in an interrogation, but they are many times crucial in negotiations.

Just as interrogation is a "role-playing" mindset, so is negotiation. Negotiators must learn to use emotions strategically to achieve the affect they need. Negotiators must have emotional intelligence—the ability to adjust their message to adapt to the other party's emotional state.[55] Interrogators use emotional intelligence to play off the subject's emotions and know which theme to pursue. Negotiators use emotional intelligence to navigate the direction of negotiations. Successful negotiators learn to read the other party and use emotion strategically throughout the course of negotiations; just as successful interrogators learn to read the subject and play off their emotions to create a win-win situation.

The role of emotions and behavior will come up again later in the paper. Up to this point, this paper discussed the difference between an interview and interrogation, outlined characteristics of successful interrogators/negotiators, and highlighted the importance of emotions and behavior in the interrogation and negotiation process. Now, the focus will be on the Reid 9-step interrogation process and the interplay negotiation has in these steps.

Step 1: The Positive Confrontation

Reid defines Step 1 as "a technique used to advise the suspect that he is without question the perpetrator of the crime."[56] This is the first step between the interview and the interrogation phase. In non-custodial environments, it's important to correctly perform this step because there is nothing keeping the subject there. The interrogator should be polite, but not too friendly, and have a confident demeanor.[57] Ideally, no more than 5-10 minutes should pass between the interview and interrogation phase because the subject's anxiety level is pretty high at the end of the interview and the interrogator wants the same level of anxiety at the start of interrogation in

14

order to keep the suspect engaged.[58] The confrontation statement should have an innuendo of evidence or a clear statement of involvement and avoid emotionally charged language. Once the statement is made, the interrogator should pause briefly to observe the subject's behavior.[59]

Similarly, in negotiation, the negotiating party can "test the waters" to see if the situation is worthy of negotiation or not. Step 1 in Reid is similar to a trial request in negotiation. In a trial request, one party makes a request to the other party.[60] This request embodies considerable power and ups the ante of the exchange to let party A know party B is not passive and party A is not in control. The trial request redefines the stakes and shakes up habitual patterns of behavior and thought to encourage creative problem solving. These factors enhance the ability for productive negotiation.[61] The positive confrontation is like interest-based negotiation. Interest-based negotiation is defined as "an approach to negotiation where the parties focus on their individual interests and the interests of the other parties to find a common ground for building a mutually acceptable agreement."[62] Cohen states people view themselves as generally good. People entering into negotiation generally see themselves as good people also. If everyone tends to see themselves as good people, then it makes sense for everyone to treat each other with the understanding they are dealing with a good person. If someone goes into a negotiation process with the intent to crush the other party, they are choosing to beat up on a party that views themselves as good people.[63] In interrogation, a subject may be guilty and be a good person. No matter what the person may have done, he or she continues to view him/herself as a good person. Using interest-based negotiation, the interrogator can identify the interests of each party. An interest is something someone needs versus what they want. The interrogator needs a confession or information. Interest-based negotiation allows greater flexibility and freedom in the decision-making process. Focusing on the interests and not positions helps to overcome differences that

15

arise between people.[64] Negotiators want to look for mutual gain by identifying shared interests. Three important things to remember about shared interests: they lie latent in every negotiation and may not be immediately obvious; they are opportunities and not godsends; and stressing shared interests can make negotiation smoother and more amicable.[65] These same three things apply to interrogation. There are shared interests in every interrogation. There are opportunities and stressing the shared interests can make interrogation smoother and more amicable. Finally, an interest-based approach leads to Step 2 in the Reid process: Interrogation Theme.

Step 2: Interrogation Theme

Reid defines Step 2: Interrogation Theme as the most important step in the 9-step process. It's defined as "a monologue presented by the interrogator in which reasons and excuses are offered that will serve to psychologically (not legally) justify, or minimize the moral seriousness of the suspect's criminal behavior."[66] During the verbal transition from Step 1 to Step 2, the interrogator changes roles from someone who is accusing the person to someone who is willing to sit and listen as to why the person did what he or she did. The theme development step is a "face-saving" step and places the blame onto someone or something other than the suspect.[67] In addition, the theme development contrasts what the suspect did to something much worse. The objective is to obtain the first admission of guilt. While proposing the theme, it's important not to ask for reasons on why the subject did something, but suggest the reasons.[68] The interrogator should maintain control of the interrogation by not allowing the suspect to make long statements or explanations. The interrogator should be mindful of the suspect's behavior once the theme is developed. If the suspect rejects the theme, their posture becomes stiff, rigid, and closed. They may have a smirk on their face and continue denials. However, if they accept the theme, the barriers may drop, there is nod of agreement, denials weaken, and the suspect may even make occasional eye contact with the interrogator.[69]

This step is similar to the "science" of exchange versus the "art" of the bargain in negotiation.[70] In order to persuade someone, the person must be tempted or motivated. A negotiator's point of view is the product they are selling and successful persuasion requires the negotiator to appeal to other's emotions.[71] The science of the exchange is the tactics and techniques used to get the sell. The art of the bargain is simply achieving the objective with deft precision and economy of effort that the other party contributes to the effort rather than resists it.[72] This same concept is effective in interrogation. The interrogator has to persuade the subject to confess. In order to do this, the subject must be tempted or motivated. The interrogator must sell their point of view to the subject. This is done through the theme development. The theme development appeals to the subject's emotion by minimizing the crime and allowing the subject to "save face." Once the interrogator appeals to the subject's emotion and buys into the theme, the subject is more inclined to contribute to the effort than to resist it. This is the ideal situation, however there are times when the subject will continuously deny guilt. This leads to Step 3: Handling Denials.

Step 3: Handling Denials

Reid defines Step 3: Handling Denials as "any statement or action that contradicts or refuses to accept the truthfulness of an allegation."[73] An interrogator wants to reduce the amount of times a suspect makes denials because each time the suspect denies their involvement in a crime, the less likely the person will tell the truth. According to Reid, it's OK to allow the first denial but the interrogator should try to discourage any further verbal or nonverbal denials. Verbal denials involve permission phases where the subject tries to interject with a statement to try and say something. Nonverbal denials come in the form of interruption gestures such as head movements, eye contact, or opening the mouth as if to say something.[74] The interrogator should discourage this behavior through a command phrase and accompanying gesture followed with an important message. For example, when the suspect begins to say something, the interrogator should state the suspect's first name and then a command phrase such as "wait," "hold it," "just a minute," etc.; along with a physical gesture such as holding up the hand or turning the head away.[75] From there, the interrogator should return to the theme immediately and keep repeating it to the suspect. If a suspect is truly innocent, the interrogator will not be allowed to get past this point because the rate of denial will be strong, firm, forceful, persistent, use descriptive language, and the suspect will continually reject the theme.[76]

Step 3 is another form of negotiation jujitsu. In negotiation jujitsu, one party avoids pitting their strength against the other party's strength directly but instead uses their skill to step aside and turn their strength to their ends. Instead of resisting the other party's force, they channel it into exploring the interests and inventing options for mutual gain.[77] A party that wants to play hardball may typically attack the other party's position forcefully; they may attack their ideas and/or they may attack the party personally. A skilled negotiator can use negotiation jujitsu to counter attacks, however the negotiator should not try to re-attack the other party. Look at it as an option and neither accept nor reject it. Try to figure out the interests behind the position, the principles in the position, and think about ways to improve the position. The next step is to not defend ideas but to invite criticism and advice.[78] If the negotiating party rejects an idea, ask them what is wrong with the idea and ask them for advice. In doing this, the other party may inadvertently derive a solution to help both party's interests. Finally, if the other party makes a personal attack, recast that attack as an attack on the problem. Two strategies in negotiation jujitsu is to ask questions instead of make statements and the use of silence when the other party makes an unreasonable proposal or unjustified attack. People are naturally uncomfortable with silence and will be compelled to break it.[79] Similar to interrogations, refusing to give up can be the most compelling persuasion. In negotiations, the persuasion of one party's point of view prevails over time through a steady, determined approach where the party refuses to take "no" for an answer.[80] If the requesting party remains calm, focused, and continues to acknowledge the other party's point of view but turns it around to the requesting point of view, the virtue of persistence prevails. A little negotiation jujitsu can be integrated into interrogation to keep the subject talking and not walking and works perfectly with the next step, overcoming objectives.

Step 4: Overcoming Objections

Step 4: Overcoming Objections is defined as "a statement that is proposed by the suspect as an excuse or a reason why the accusation is false."[81] The key to this step is to turn the objection around and use it as a reason why the suspect should tell the truth. [82] The objection can be used to further develop a theme or to refine the current theme. Aside from negotiation jujitsu, a power negotiating tactic and technique is to actually uncover an objection and use it as leverage for the negotiation.[83] In interrogations, if the interrogator recognizes the objection, they can draw it out and accept most of the objections with a statement of agreement or understanding. The interrogator can discuss the positive and negative aspects of the suspect's objection and continue to play on the theme. If the interrogator handles the objections successfully, the subject may start to feel they have no control of the situation and start to withdraw from the interrogation. Overcoming objections in negotiation, coupled with the art of persuasion and persistence, can wear the other party down and increase their likelihood of reaching an amicable solution. The caution to wearing down the other party is they may start to retreat, emotionally withdraw, or become inattentive. If this starts to happen, step 5 must be enacted quickly.

Step 5: Procurement and Retention of Suspect's Attention

The closer the interrogator gets to the truth, the suspect may start to pull back and psychologically withdraw. The suspect begins to tune the interrogator out and starts to focus on the consequences of telling the truth. The interrogator must act quickly to keep the suspect's attention. During psychological withdrawal, the suspect is quiet but not really listening. The suspect begins to put up emotional barriers and may appear emotionally uninvolved. The interrogator needs to pull the suspect back in and can do this by physically moving closer to the suspect, establish eye contact, and get the suspect emotionally and mentally involved.[84] The interrogator must be careful not to move so close to the suspect that it becomes a threat. It's at this point many interrogators start to give up. Interrogators, just like negotiators, must continue to be persistent and finish the race. Interrogators should keep repeating the theme, but remember to keep the even, calm tone and not let frustration take over.

As stated earlier, non-verbal communication plays a key role in interrogation and negotiation. If a suspect is guilty, they will have a hard time looking the interrogator in the eye. If a negotiating party is deceptive, they will have a hard time looking the other party in the eye. Negotiating parties should ensure they establish eye contact because it's a way to show attentiveness and interest. In the art of persuasion, it's important to make eye contact when delivering the most important part of the message.[85] It's also important to maintain eye contact even when the negotiator is listening. Through eye contact, the negotiator can indicate acceptance or non-acceptance of an idea, and can also encourage or discourage what the other party says. Finally, in order to maintain communication and keep the other party interested, body language should indicate interest. To show attentiveness, the negotiator should hold their body erect, lean slightly forward, and face the other person directly.[86] This is the same type of posture the interrogator should use when dealing with the suspect. In either case, if the other party senses disinterest, they will be more likely to retreat and lose interest in the negotiation or the interrogation. This may lead to a passive mood in the suspect or the other negotiating party and potentially lead to a stalemate.

Step 6: Handling Suspect's Passive Mood

This step could indicate a turning point in the interrogation process. In Step 6: Handling Suspect's Passive Mood, the suspect is mentally debating whether or not to tell the truth. Some suspects become overwhelmed with guilt and remorse, while others just simply give up and decide to tell the truth.[87] The non-verbal signs described in the previous steps which hinder negotiations are the signs of defeat displayed by suspects. For example, the suspect may become more relaxed and less tense. The suspect may slump in their chair or hold their head down. They may take a deep sigh of resignation and may even start to cry. The interrogator can comment on this behavior, move closer to the subject, and offer the alternative (discussed in the next step).[88]

During negotiations, framing is about focusing, shaping, and organizing the world or making sense out of complexities and put it in an understandable concept.[89] As negotiations evolve, the frame of the issue may change. The conversation exchange between the parties is what shapes the frame. Lewicki et al offers prescriptive advice with regards to negotiation framing: parties frame the issues that are important to them in the view they want the other party to see; both negotiating parties have their own frames; frames are controllable; throughout the negotiation, frames may change in a way the negotiator cannot predict but may be able to control; and certain frames can lead to certain outcomes.[90] In the framing process, one party wants the other party to see their point of view. If the other party does not view the issue in the same light, the negotiating party may need to reframe. The frame can define major shifts and transitions in the negotiation. Interests, rights, and power are three frame approaches commonly used in negotiation.[91] Interests are where people are concerned about what they need, desire, or want. Rights are where people are concerned about what is right, correct, or fair. Power is where people are concerned about power over the other person.[92] Depending on how the issue is framed will determine the outcome. Framing in an interrogation setting is effective in step 6 at the point where the suspect starts to surrender. Framing is also an effective measure leading up to step 7: presenting the alternative question.

Step 7: Presenting the Alternative Question

Step 7 is the 2nd most important step in Reid's 9-step process. This is considered the climax to theme development and is all about saving face. The alternative question is defined as, "a question asked of the suspect, in which the suspect is offered two incriminating choices concerning some aspect of the crime. Accepting either choice represents the first admission of guilt. Of course, the suspect always has a third option of rejecting both choices and simply denying any involvement in the offense."[93] The key to the alternative question is either choice is an admission of guilt, but one choice sounds better than the other and allows the suspect to save face. The interrogator should have a desirable and undesirable alternative and then a positive or negative supporting statement. The supporting statement is an extension of one of the alternative questions and subtly encourages the suspect to choose one of the alternatives.[94] For example, the interrogator may ask, "has this happened several times before, or is this just the first time? This is the first time isn't it?"[95] For this step to be successful, the interrogator must keep presenting

22

the alternative and supporting statement to encourage the suspect to choose one. In other words, the interrogator is making sense out of complexities and putting it in an understandable concept, or using framing to get an admission of guilt. According to the Reid Technique, the way this step works is an innocent person will not confess to a crime just because the interrogator presents two scenarios and one sounds better than the other. If the interrogator is truly sincere, or at least appears to be sincere, most likely a guilty person will concede and respond to the alternative.[96]

Negotiation has a similar concept. It's called the Best Alternative to a Negotiated Agreement (BATNA). The BATNA is not the bottom line of a negotiation but is a measure of balance of power among the negotiating parties based on the resources they control or influence.[97] The balance of power does not guarantee the outcome of the negotiation, but helps to shape the negotiation. If one party needs something more than the other, then the balance of power is tilted and that party with less of a need can use power to influence the negotiation. Each time new information is revealed, the BATNA can change. Fisher & Ury state there are three distinct operations in generating BATNAs: 1) a list of actions one might take if no agreement is reached; 2) improving some of the more promising ideas and converting them into suitable alternatives; and 3) selecting one of the alternatives that seems best.[98] Each option given at the negotiation table should be weighed against the BATNA. Parties that enter into negotiations with a clearly established and viable BATNA bring more power to the negotiation. These parties know what they will and will not accept and it enables the party to make a decision on the proposed offer. Suspects under interrogation have BATNAs and interrogators have BATNAs. Guilty suspects can continue to play the game of denial or determine it's better to confess and get the weight off their chest. Interrogators know their BATNA going in and use this BATNA to determine theme development. Interrogators use BATNA again when the suspect continues to resist telling the truth. The alternative seals the deal in the interrogation and the BATNA determines whether an issue is worth negotiating or not. If it works and the interrogator gets an admission of guilt, the next step is to get the details of the offense.

Step 8: Having Suspect Orally Relate the Various Details of the Offense

Once the suspect chooses one of the alternatives, it's the first step to an admission or confession. The interrogator should give a statement of encouragement to the suspect for taking the first step and should then start to get the details of the offense.[99] At this point, the interrogator is back to an interview technique where the suspect does most of the talking. The interrogator asks questions to get the details and information surrounding the crime, or to elicit intelligence as in the military cases. It is important for the interrogator to give the suspect their full attention and not to write any notes until the full confession is offered. Note-taking distracts the suspect and can even make the suspect retreat and stop talking. The interrogator must continue to have patience and let the suspect give the details at their own pace.

After hours, days, or even months of negotiation, this is what each party wants to see: agreement. It's important for the parties to recap all the details of the agreement to ensure each party knows what they agreed to. Details are important because seemingly small details that don't get ironed out have a way of coming back as bigger issues in the long run. Closing the deal is the 6th phase in the 7 phases of negotiation and is geared toward building the commitment to the agreed upon solution.[100] Once the details of the offense or agreement are verbalized, it's time to move to the final step: written documentation.

Step 9: Converting an Oral Confession into a Written Confession

After all the hard work of getting an admission of guilt or confession, the interrogator wants to put pen to paper and get everything the suspect said in writing. Written confessions hold more weight than oral confessions. There are four types of written confessions an interrogator may use: a statement written by the suspect; a statement written by the interrogator; a formal statement; or a video/tape recorded confession.[101] The interrogator should get the written confession as soon as possible after the oral confession to prevent any incongruence in the stories. The written confession signals the end of the interrogation. In negotiation, a handshake, written agreement, press release, or contract signals the end of the negotiation. The documents serve as legally binding and hold each party accountable for those items of agreement. Something to keep in mind in negotiating is to ensure the party making the agreement has the authority to do so. A party may act on behalf of a company or agency but may not have the authority to enter into a formal agreement. These details should all become clear during the closing discussions. If the representative does not have the authority to enter into a formal agreement, then written documentation should be drawn and it should discuss each item agreed to during the negotiating process. Set a date for the other party to respond and pursue the written agreement in that fashion.

Conclusion

Former President Jimmy Carter highlighted five key points in *Negotiation: An Alternative to Hostility*. The keys to effective negotiation is 1) all parties must be convinced the issues can and should be settled; 2) overt pressure to force others to negotiate is often counterproductive; 3) agreement must be ultimately mutually derived; 4) repeated analysis of current circumstances will most often reveal opportunities for progress; and 5) proper forum is needed, and negotiators must be known to have authority to conclude agreements.[102] This same concept can be applied to interrogations. In interrogation, 1) both parties must be convinced it is better to tell the truth than to lie; 2) overt pressure to force the suspect to tell the truth is often counterproductive; 3) confession must be ultimately unanimous; 4) repeated analysis of tactics and techniques will often reveal opportunities for progress; and 5) proper forum is needed (privacy) and interrogations should only be conducted by trained interrogators.

The US does not need to continue to live in the darkness of the Abu Ghraib or GITMO accusations of abuse and torture. This paper discussed the background of these two incidents and its treatment of detainees. It then discussed the differences between an interview and interrogation and looked at some of the characteristics, environment, behavior and emotions present in interviews, interrogations, and negotiations. In addition, this paper briefly analyzed each step of the Reid 9-steps of interrogation and correlated each step to negotiation. Through these examples, it's clear that interrogation and negotiation are related and it's possible to incorporate negotiation theory and processes into interrogation and get good results. If the reader is still not convinced, here is one last example.

Matthew Alexander, the US interrogator who took down Abu Musab al Zarqawi, detailed the steps he used to extract the critical information to find this most wanted man. Several other interrogators tried for months to get Abu Haydar to talk. He would not say a word. Matthew decided to go against the grain and try something different. He used a negotiation strategy. He first played to Haydar's ego and then built rapport through a common topic: religion. Matthew started asking about Islam and then discussed Iraqi history. According to Haydar, this is the first time an American was interested in hearing about Islam. Over the course of several hours, Matthew was able to gain a key piece of intelligence needed to lead the Special Forces to Zarqawi. Matthew gained Abu Haydar's trust through respect and courtesy. Not one time did he use any kind of harsh technique to extract information.[103] If this "kindler, gentler" technique can work against Al Qaida, it can certainly work for everyone else.

In negotiation, long term relationships are critical for future business relationships. In interrogation, there is less emphasis on establishing long term relationships. However, in negotiation and interrogation, some sort of trust relationship must be established in order to get the results one wants: agreement and/or confession. This is another example of the similarity between negotiation and interrogations. The Reid Technique for interrogation holds useful tools for a negotiator to add to their toolbox, and negotiation theories are useful tools for the interrogator to add to their toolbox. As leaders in the military, Reid's 9 steps are useful in analyzing or solving a problem. Negotiation is something leaders do everyday and the purpose of this paper was to align two seemingly dissimilar concepts. Further analysis of this concept is likely to prove or disprove the theory negotiation and interrogation are interrelated. However, in the meantime, the theory still stands: negotiation and interrogation share similar concepts and ideas; and incorporation of negotiation theory and practice into interrogation settings will yield better results.

[1] Reid & Associates, *Reid Technique*, 94

[2] Ibid, 5

[3] FM 2-22.3, *Human Intelligence Collector Operations*, 1-8

[4] Rule, *The Art of Negotiation*, 5

[5] Cohen, *Negotiating Skills for Managers*, 3

[6] Breslin & Rubin, *Negotiation Theory and Practice*, 147

[7] "Profile: Guantanamo Bay," BBC Print News, 17 Oct 06

[8] "US Interrogation Policy Condemned," BBC Print News, 18 Jun 08

[9] DOD News Release, 596-04, 22 Jun 04

[10] The Times, 24 Jun 04

[11] Ibid.

[12] Ibid.

[13] Action Memo, 2 Dec 02

[14] The Tiimes, 24 Jun 04

[15] AR 15-6, Investigation of the Abu Ghraib Prison, 7-10

[16] Ibid, 44

[17] Ibid, 7

[18] Taylor, "How to Break a Human Being," Focus, 27

[19] Alexander, *How to Break a Terrorist*, 5

[20] Reid & Associates, *Reid Technique*, 3

[21] Ibid.

[22] FM 2-22.3, *Human Intelligence*, 8-3,4

[23] Ibid.

[24] Ibid.

[25] Shister, *10 Minute Guide to Negotiating*, 38

[26] Ibid.

[27] Lewicki, Barry, and Saunders, *Essentials of Negotiation*, 104-107

[28] Cohen, *Negotiating Skills for Managers*, 76

[29] Ibid.

[30] Ibid.

[31] Reid & Associates, *Reid Technique*, 4

[32] Walker & Harris, *Negotiations Six Steps to Success*, 1

[33] Rule, *The Art of Negotiation*, 10-12; Lewis, *Power Negotiating*, 141-152; Reid & Associates, *Reid Technique*, 3-4

[34] Vessel, "Conducting Successful Interrogations," 2

[35] Ibid.

[36] Mulbar, *Interrogation*, 12

[37] Reid & Associates, *Reid Technique*, notes

[38] Ibid.

[39] Ibid, 7

[40] Ibid, 11

[41] Ibid, 10

[42] Reid & Associates, *Reid Technique*, 10-20

[43] Nierenberg and Calero, *How to Read*, 60,74,80,92,118

[44] Cohen, *Negotiating Skills for Managers*, 107

[45] Ibid.

[46] Ibid.

[47] Shapiro, "Negotiating Emotions," 69

[48] Ibid.

[49] Ibid.

[50] Lewicki, Barry, and Saunders, *Essentials of Negotiation*, 27
[51] Ibid.
[52] Shapiro, "Negotiating Emotions," 70
[53] Ibid.
[54] Ibid.
[55] Ibid, 131
[56] Reid & Associates, *Reid Technique*, 44
[57] Ibid.
[58] Ibid, notes
[59] Ibid, 45
[60] Shister, *10-Minute Guide*, 22
[61] Ibid.
[62] Cohen, *Negotiating Skills for Managers*, 5
[63] Ibid, 6
[64] Ibid, 9
[65] Fisher & Ury, *Getting to YES*, 73
[66] Reid & Associates, *Reid Technique*, 48
[67] Ibid.
[68] Ibid, 49
[69] Ibid.
[70] Shister, *10-Minute Guide*, 24
[71] Ibid, 25
[72] Ibid, 28
[73] Reid & Associates, *Reid Technique*, 61
[74] Ibid,62
[75] Ibid.
[76] Ibid, 65
[77] Fisher & Ury, *Getting to YES*, 108
[78] Ibid.
[79] Ibid, 111-112
[80] Shister, *10-Minute Guide*, 24
[81] Reid & Associates, *Reid Technique*, 66
[82] Hartwig et al., "Police Interrogations", 383
[83] Lewis, *Power Negotiating*, 141
[84] Reid & Associates, *Reid Technique*, 70
[85] Lewicki, Barry, and Saunders, *Essentials of Negotiation*, 139
[86] Ibid
[87] Reid & Associates, *Reid Technique*, 72
[88] Ibid.
[89] Lewicki, Barry, and Saunders, *Essentials of Negotiation*, 121
[90] Ibid.
[91] Ibid.
[92] Ibid.
[93] Reid & Associates, *Reid Technique*, 73
[94] Ibid, 74
[95] Ibid.
[96] Ibid, 75.
[97] Cohen, *Negotiating Skills for Managers*, 24
[98] Fisher & Ury, *Getting to YES*, 103
[99] Reid & Associates, *Reid Technique*, 78
[100] Lewicki, Barry, and Saunders, *Essentials of Negotiation*, 94
[101] Reid & Associates, *Reid Technique*, 81
[102] Carter, *Negotiation: An Alternative to Hostility*, 20-21
[103] Alexander, *How to Break A Terrorist*, 222-270

Bibliography

Alexander, Matthew. *How To Break a Terrorist*. Free Press, New York, 2008.

Anderson, Kare. *Getting What You Want: How to Reach Agreement and Resolve Conflict Every Time.* New York, Dutton, 1993.

Aquino, Karl and Becker, Thomas E. "Lying in Negotiations: How Individual and Situational Factors Influence the Use of Neutralization Strategies." *Journal of Organizational Behavior* 26:661-679 September 2005. http://search.ebscohost.com/login.aspx?direct=true&db=bth&an=17888549

Breslin, John W., and Rubin, Jeffrey Z. *Negotiation Theory and Practice.* Cambridge, MA, Program on Negotiation at Harvard Law School, 1999.

Calero, Henry H. *Winning the Negotiation.* New York, Hawthorn Books, 1979.

Carter, Jimmy. *Negotiation, the Alternative to Hostility.* Macon, GA, Mercer University Press, 1984.

Cohen, Steven. *Negotiating Skills For Managers.* New York, NY: McGraw-Hill, 2002.

Curhan, Jared R. and Pentland, Alex. "Thin Slices of Negotiation: Predicting Outcomes from Conversational Dynamics Within the First Five Minutes." *Journal of Applied Psychology,* Vol. 92, pp. 802-811, 2007. http://ssrn.com/abstract=973827

Elfenbein, Hillary Anger, Foo, Maw Der, White, Judith B. , Tan, Hwee Hoon and Aik, Voon-Chuan. "Reading Your Counterpart: The Benefit of Emotion Recognition Accuracy for Effectiveness in Negotiation." August 25, 2006. http://ssrn.com/abstract=926577

Field Manual No. 2-22.3. *Human Intelligence Collector Operations*, 6 September 2006.

Fisher, Roger and Ury, William. *Getting to YES.* New York, Penguin Group, 1981.

Gardner, Frank. "US Bides Its Time in Guantanamo." *BBC News*, 24 August 2002. http://news.bbc.co.uk/2/hi/programmes/from_our_own_correspondent/2212874.stm

Gebhardt. James F. "The Road to Abu Ghraib: U.S. Army Detainee Doctrine and Experience." *Military Review*, January-February 2005, 44-50.

Hartwig, Maria. "Police Interrogation from a Social Psychology Perspective." Policing & Society 15, no. 4 (December 2005): 379-399

Lewicki, Roy J., Barry, Bruce, and Saunders, David M. *Essentials of Negotiation*, 4th Edition. New York, NY: McGraw-Hill, 2007.

Lewis, David V. *Power Negotiating Tactics and Techniques*. Englewood Cliffs, NJ, Prentice-Hall, 1981.

Li, Shu and Roloff, Michael. "Strategic Negative Emotion in Negotiation." June 15, 2004. IACM 17th Annual Conference Paper. http://ssrn.com/abstract=609283

Malhotra, Deepak. "Making Threats Credible." *Negotiation* 8:1-4 March 2005. http://search.ebscohost.com/login.aspx?direct=true&db=bth&AN=16277872

McRae, Brad. "The Seven Strategies of Master Negotiators." *Ivey Business Journal* 69:1-8 May-June 2005.
http://search.ebscohost.com/login.aspx?direct=true&db=bth&an=17557096

Mulbar, Harold. *Interrogation*. Illinois, Bannerstone House, 1951.

Nierenberg, Gerard and Calero, Henry. *How to Read a Person Like a Book*, New York, NY, Fall River Press, 1993.

Orecklin, Michele. "Why They Crack." *Time* 161, no. 26 (30 June 2003): 29-31.

Raiffa, Howard. *The Art and Science of Negotiation.* Cambridge, MA, Belknap Press of Harvard University Press, 1982.

Reid, John E. & Associates. *The Reid Technique of Interviewing and Interrogation*. Seminar Coursebook. Illinois, 2008.

Reuters. "Profile: Guantanamo Bay." *BBC News*, 17 October 2006. http://news.bbc.co.uk/2/hi/americas/4720962.stm

Reuters. "US Interrogation Policy Condemned." *BBC News*, 18 June 2008. http://news.bbc.co.uk/2/hi/americas/7460444.stm

Reuters. "Tipton Three Complains of Beatings." *BBC News*. 14 March 2004. http://news.bbc.co.uk/2/hi/uk_news/3509750.stm

Richardson, Stephen, Dohrenwend, Barbara and Klein, David. *Interviewing*. New York, Basic Books, Inc. 1965.

Ripley, Amanda and others. "The Rules of Interrogation." *Time* 163, no. 20 (17 May 2004): 44-46.

Rule, Gordon Wade. *The Art of Negotiation*. Self-published. 1962.

Rumsfeld, Donald. To The Commander, US Southern Command. Memorandum, 16 Apr 2003.

Salacuse, Jeswald W. "Your Place or Mine? Deciding Where to Negotiate." *Negotiation* 8:7-9 April 2005.
http://search.ebscohost.com/login.aspx?direct=true&db=bth&AN=16696341

Schweitzer, Maurice E. "Call Their Bluff! Detecting Deception in Negotiation." *Negotiation* 10:7-9 March 2007.
http://search.ebscohost.com/login.aspx?direct=true&db=bth&AN=24198911

Schweitzer, Maurice E. "Negotiators Lie." *Negotiation* 8:1-4 December 2005.
http://search.ebscohost.com/login.aspx?direct=true&db=bth&AN=19047871

Shapiro, Daniel L. "Negotiating Emotions." *Conflict Resolution Quarterly* 20:67-82 Fall 2002. http://search.ebscohost.com/login.aspx?direct=true&db=aph&an=9132004

Shapiro, Daniel L. "Teaching Students How to Use Emotions as They Negotiate." *Negotiation Journal* 22:105-109 January 2006.
http://search.ebscohost.com/login.aspx?direct=true&db=bth&an=19398142

Shister, Neil. *10 Minute Guide to Negotiating.* New York, Alpha Books, 1997.

Smithey Fulmer, Ingrid and Barry, Bruce, "Lying and Smiling: Informational and Emotional Deception in Negotiation." *Journal of Business Ethics, Forthcoming.* 1 April 2007.
http://ssrn.com/abstract=962518

Taylor, Ian. "Interrogation: How to Break a Human Being." *Focus.* #192, Summer 2008, 22-29.

Tenbrunsel, Ann E. and Diekmann, Kristina A. "When You're Tempted to Deceive." *Negotiation* 10:9-11 July 2007.
http://search.ebscohost.com/login.aspx?direct=true&db=bth&AN=25581814

Vessel, David. "Conducting Successful Interrogations." *FBI Law Enforcement Bulletin* 67, no. 10 (October 1998): 1-6.

Walker, Michael A. and Harris, George L. *Negotiations: Six Steps to Success.* Upper Saddle River, NJ, PTR Prentice Hall, 1995.

Wheeler, Michael. "Do You Know Where to Look for the Right Cue?" *Negotiation,* pp 3-5, December 2003.
http://search.ebscohost.com/login.aspx?direct=true&db=bth&AN=13520194

Wind, Bruce A. "A Guide to Crisis Negotiations." *FBI Law Enforcement Bulletin* 64:7-12 October 1995. http://proquest.umi.com/pqdweb?did=8670257&Fmt=7&clientId=417&RQT=309&VName=PQD

Zartman, William I. *The 50% Solution: How to Bargain Successfully with Hijackers, Strikers, Bosses, Oil Magnates, Arabs, Russians and Other Worthy Opponents in This Modern World.* New Haven, CT, Yale University Press, 1987.

Zartman, William I. *The Negotiation Process: Theories and Applications.* Beverly Hills, CA, Sage Publications, 1978.

www.ingramcontent.com/pod-product-compliance
Lightning Source LLC
Chambersburg PA
CBHW080734290526
45790CB00008B/3184